The Dwarfs

adapted from Harold Pinter's novel of the same name

Harold Pinter was born in London in 1930. He is married to Antonia Fraser. In 1995 he won the David Cohen British Literature Prize, awarded for a lifetime's achievement in literature. In 1996 he was given the Laurence Olivier Award for a lifetime's achievement in theatre.

Kerry Lee Crabbe has worked extensively as a writer, producer and director in film, theatre and television. For Granada he adapted Tennessee Williams's *Cat on a Hot Tin Roof*, produced by and starring Laurence Olivier. He has written five original screenplays, including *The Playboys* for the Goldwyn Company starring Albert Finney. He was nominated Most Promising Playwright by the Evening Standard for his stage play *Rough Magic*. His adaptation of *The Dwarfs*, a novel by Harold Pinter, was screened on BBC4 in October 2002.

by Harold Pinter

plays
ASHES TO ASHES
BETRAYAL
THE BIRTHDAY PARTY
THE CARETAKER
CELEBRATION and THE ROOM
THE COLLECTION and THE LOVER
THE HOMECOMING
HOTHOUSE
MOONLIGHT
PRESS CONFERENCE
THE ROOM and THE DUMB WAITER

PLAYS ONE
(The Birthday Party, The Room, The Dumb Waiter, A Slight Ache,
The Hothouse, A Night Out, The Black and White, The Examination)

PLAYS TWO
(The Caretaker, The Dwarfs, The Collection, The Lover, Night School,
Trouble in the Works, Request Stop, Last to Go, Special Offer)

PLAYS THREE
(The Homecoming, Tea Party, The Basement, Landscape, Silence, Night,
That's Your Trouble, That's All, Applicant, Interview, Dialogue for Three,
Tea Party (short story), Old Times, No Man's Land)

PLAYS FOUR
(Betrayal, Monologue, One for the Road, Mountain Language,
Family Voices, A Kind of Alaska, Victoria Station, Precisely,
The New World Order, Party Time, Moonlight, Ashes to Ashes)

screenplays
HAROLD PINTER COLLECTED SCREENPLAYS ONE
(The Servant, The Pumpkin Eater, The Quiller Memorandum,
Accident, The Last Tycoon, Langrishe, Go Down)
HAROLD PINTER COLLECTED SCREENPLAYS TWO
(The Go-Between, The Proust Screenplay, Victory, Turtle Diary, Reunion)
HAROLD PINTER COLLECTED SCREENPLAYS THREE
(The French Lieutenant's Woman, The Heat of the Day,
The Comfort of Strangers, The Trial, The Dreaming Child)

poetry and prose
COLLECTED POEMS AND PROSE
THE DWARFS (a novel)
100 POEMS BY 100 POETS
99 POEMS IN TRANSLATION
VARIOUS VOICES: Prose, Poetry, Politics 1948–1998

The Dwarfs

Kerry Lee Crabbe

adapted from the novel by
Harold Pinter

ff
faber and faber

This adaptation first published in 2003
by Faber and Faber Limited
3 Queen Square London WC1N 3AU

Typeset by Country Setting, Kingsdown, Kent CT14 8ES
Printed in England by Intype Libra Limited

All rights reserved
Original novel © Harold Pinter, 1990
Adaptation © Kerry Lee Crabbe, 2003

The right of Kerry Lee Crabbe to be identified as author
of this work has been asserted in accordance with Section 77
of the Copyright, Designs and Patents Act 1988

All rights whatsoever in this work, amateur or professional,
are strictly reserved. Applications for permission for any use
whatsoever including professional performance rights
must be made in advance, prior to any such proposed use,
to Judy Daish Associates, 2 St Charles Place, London W10 6EG.
No performance may be given unless a licence has first
been obtained.

*This book is sold subject to the condition that it shall not, by way
of trade or otherwise, be lent, resold, hired out or otherwise
circulated without the publisher's prior consent in any form of
binding or cover other than that in which it is published and
without a similar condition including this condition being
imposed on the subsequent purchaser*

A CIP record for this book
is available from the British Library

ISBN 0-571-22104-1

The Dwarfs, in this adaptation, was first presented on stage at the Tricycle Theatre, London, on 17 April 2003, with the following cast:

Pete Jamie Lee
Len Mark Rice-Oxley
Mark Ben Caplan
Virginia Daisy Haggard

Directed by Christopher Morahan
Designed by Eileen Diss
Lighting by Mick Hughes

Characters

Len
Pete
Mark
Virginia

All the characters are in their early twenties

The action takes place
in East London in 1950

Act One

I

Mark's place. Enter Len and Pete.

Pete Well, everything looks in good order.

Len It's like the workhouse here.
You'd think a man like him would have a maid, wouldn't you, to look after the place while he's away? Or a gentleman. A gentleman's gentleman. Are you quite sure he hasn't got a gentleman's gentleman tucked away somewhere to look after the place for him?

Pete Only you. You're the only gentleman's gentleman he's got.

Len If I'm his gentleman's gentleman, I should have been looking after the place for him.

From his inside pocket Len draws out a recorder. He blows into it, holds it up to the light and puts it to his mouth. There is no sound.

Pete Don't overdo it.

Len taps the recorder on his head.

Len What's the matter with it?
There's something wrong with this recorder.
I can't do a thing with it.

Pete looks around the room.

Len Everything in this house is Portuguese.

Pete Why's that?

Len That's where he comes from.

Pete So he does.

Len Or at least, his grandfather on his mother's side.

Pete Well, well.

Len Or his grandmother on his father's side.

A distant clock chimes.

Pete What time is he coming?

Len About half past one.

Len fiddles with his recorder.

Pete What's the matter with that thing?

Len There's nothing wrong with it. It's the best on the market. But it must be broken. It's a year since I played it.

Pete stands up and strolls to the bookshelf. On the bottom shelf he finds a Bible.

Pete I gave him this, years ago.

Len What?

Pete This Bible.

Len What for?

Pete pushes the book back and brushes his fingers,

Pete What about a shot of air?

Len Not me.

Pete Why not?

Len No, I know where you'll drag me.

Pete Where?

Len Over the Lea.

Pete Well?

Len You don't know what it's like there at night.

Pete Don't I?

Len inspects his glasses.

Len It's still there.

Pete What now?

Len You don't know what you're missing by not wearing glasses.

Pete What am I missing?

Len I'll tell you. You see, there's always a point of light in the centre of the lens, in the centre of your sight. You can't go wrong. What this point of light does, it indicates the angle of your orbit. There's no need to look at me like that.

Pete Do I have to go down on my bended knees?

Len I'm giving you a hot tip.

Len sits.

Ten to one he'll be hungry.

Pete Why?

Len I'll lay odds.

Pete closes his eyes.

He can eat like a bullock, that bloke. Of course he may have changed. (*Standing up and moving around the room.*) Things do change. But I'm the same. Do you know I had five solid square meals one day last week. At eleven o'clock, two o'clock, six o'clock, ten o'clock and one o'clock. Not bad going. I'm always starving when I get up. Daylight has a funny effect on me. As for the night, that goes without saying. As far as I'm concerned the only thing you can do in the night is eat. It keeps me fit, especially if I'm at home. I have to run upstairs to put the kettle on, run 'tairs to finish what I'm doing, run upstairs to cut a sandwich or arrange a salad, run downstairs to finish what I'm doing, run back upstairs to see to the sausages, if I'm having sausages, run back downstairs to finish what I'm doing, run back upstairs –

Pete Yes!

Len Where did you get those shoes?

Pete What?

Len Those shoes. How long have you had them?

Pete Why, what's the matter with them?

Len I'm losing my grip. Have you been wearing them all night?

Pete No. I walked from Bethnal Green in my naked feet.

Len I must be losing my grip.

He sits.

Pete When did you last sleep?

Len Sleep? All I do is sleep. It's best on night shift. The trains come in, I give a bloke half a dollar, he does my job, I curl up in a corner and read the timetables. But they tell me I've got the makings of a number one porter . . . What are you doing with your hand?

Pete What do you think I'm doing with it, eh?

Len I don't know.

Pete I'll tell you, shall I? Nothing. I'm not doing anything with it.

Len You're holding it palm upwards.

Pete What about it?

Len It's not normal. Let's have a look at that hand. Let's have a look at it. (*He gasps through his teeth.*) You're a homicidal maniac.

Pete Is that a fact?

Len Look. Look at that hand. Straight line right across the middle, see? Horizontal. You're a nut.

The bell rings.

Pete That's the man. Open the door.

Mark (*off*) Anyone there?

Len Coming! (*He exits.*) Hello, Mark.

The figure of Mark appears in the doorway.

II

Virginia, isolated in a pool of light.

Virginia Pete's father is dead. The police thought it was suicide. More likely, Pete said, he'd been drunk and left the gas on. He was flat out on the carpet. Pete had been in the kitchen, mending the sink. He stayed with the body for twenty minutes. The spanner was still in his hand. All this emotion business, he said – what is it? A load of old bubbles, blown down the coal-hole. He could have easily gone back and finished mending the sink.

His father was as dead as a crusty old ant. And as for Pete . . . He couldn't give two pins to the dressmaker for the whole business.

III

Len's place. Len at the table, with a writing pad and a book. A knock at the door. Len admits Mark.

Len Did you get any sleep?

Mark I slept all day.

Len Come in.
What do you think of my kitchen? Has it changed?

Mark It remains a kitchen of the highest possible class.

Len What do you think of this book?

Mark Reimann's *Theory of Integrals*? What are you trying to do, lead me into temptation?

Len Why don't you read it? There's nothing like a bit of calculus to cheer you up.

Mark What's this? (*Lifting a piece of paper from between the pages.*)

Len What is it?

Mark It's one of your poems.

Len snatches it, reads it quickly and crumples it into his pocket.

What's the matter?

Len It's gibberish.

Mark What about Pete? Has he been writing anything lately?

Len How would I know? It's not my business. But he's got other kettles on the boil.

Mark I wonder what they are?

Len You're entitled to wonder.

Mark looks around the room.

Mark The rooms we live in.

Len Don't tell me, don't mention it. The rooms we live in open and shut. They change shape at their own will.

Mark Well, there's only one thing I've got to say.

Len What's that?

Mark When you're in, you're in.

Len What? What did you say? When you're in, you're in?

Mark Sure.

Len You're right. I can't deny it. You've never said a truer word.

Len attempts to play his recorder.

It's an insult to Bach! The trouble is that when I find some direction for my energies I can't sustain it. I've been a farmhand, a builder's mate, a packer, a stagehand, a shipping clerk, I've dug turf, I've been a hop picker, a salesman, a postman, I'm a railway porter, a mathematician, a musician, I scribble and I play a fair game of cricket. I haven't touched pearl-diving and I've never been a male nurse. What sort of set-up's that? It's ludicrous. I've never been able to look in the mirror and say, this is me.

Mark Ah, well.

Len Do you know, I'm never quite sure that you understand one word I'm talking about. I sometimes get the impression that you do nothing but study form. Pete, for instance, will always let me know when he doesn't understand what I'm saying, in one way or another. He feels it's a moral duty. You rarely do that. What does that mean? Does it mean that you never want to commit yourself? Or does it mean that you've got nothing to commit?

Mark Were you saying something?

Pause.

Len Where were you acting? Huddersfield?

Mark That's right.

Len Did they like you in Huddersfield?

Mark They loved me.

Len What's it like when you act? Does it please you? Does it please anyone else?

Mark What's wrong with acting?

Len It's a time-honoured profession. It goes without saying. But what does it do? (*Sighs.*)
Do you know what I am? I'm an agent for a foreign power.

The doorbell rings.

Pete (*off*) Well, come on, let me in.

Len lets Pete in.

Why don't you switch on a few lights? This place is like the black hole of Calcutta. (*To Mark*) What ho.

Mark Greetings.

Pete What about a shake in the air? You both look as if you could do with it.

Mark You're right. Let's get out.

Len Perhaps you'd like to hear a little serenade before you go. It's by Spack and Rutz and played by Yetta Clatta. It's church music.

Pete Another time, Weinblatt.

They leave.

IV

Street. Pete, Len and Mark walking.

Len Listen here, Pete. Why do you always call me Weinblatt? My name's Weinstein. Always has been.

Pete It won't stick.

Mark coughs, and spits copiously.

Mark . . . you're out on your own as a gobber.

Mark 'Man stands amazed to see his deformity
In any other creature but himself!'

Pete 'Thou art a box of worm-seed; at best, but a salvatory of green mummy.'

Mark Thanks.

Len I've signed my name to something.

Mark Joined the army?

Len No. I've applied for a job in an insurance office.

Mark Don't say that.

Len I know what'll happen. They'll have me doing mortality tables all day.

Pete You could stick it, with a bit of go and guts.

Mark It's no joke, this job business.

Len Well, it all depends on which way you look at it. For instance, I know a geezer who's always touching wood. So, you know what he did? He took a job in a library. Look at all the chances there are for touching wood in a library. The place is full of wood. He has the time of his life. (*He checks his watch.*) I'm on the night shift.

Mark 'We are now upon parting.'

Pete 'You are for Milan?'

Len No. Euston.

Pete So go and catch your bus.

Len leaves. Pete and Mark resume walking.

Do you know what he's up to?

Mark No. What?

Pete He's started to read the New Testament.

Mark And the very best of luck. (*He sniffs.*) Where's the factory?

Pete (*sniffing*) Somewhere over there. Day and night they let out that stink. Straight into my bedroom window.

They turn their collars up against a gust of rain.

Listen. What do you know about love?

Mark Love?

Pete Yes, you must know something about it.

Mark What makes you say that?

They take shelter.

Pete It sticks out a mile you're the right bloke to ask about love.

Mark Does it? Why?

Pete The point is this. I've got a few ideas for some love stories for women's magazines.

Mark You're pulling my whatsit.

Pete Cross my heart, I'm not. Well, come on. What's it all about?

Mark Do me a favour.

Pete What's the matter? You've been up to your knees in this love lark for years.

Mark That's right. It makes the world go round.

Pete How does a bloke in love feel? What are his feelings?

Mark Look, why don't you find out for yourself?

Pete How do I go about it?

The rain eases. They emerge from their shelter.

Mark All right. You've brought it up. What's the position between you and Virginia?

Pete We've got a lot in common.

Mark But you wouldn't say you loved her?

Pete That question might even be relevant. But I can't answer it.

Mark Does the blood flow?

Pete What do you mean?

Mark Does it flow?

Pete The blood? Well, I'll tell you. We don't go in for it much these days.

Mark You don't?

Pete No. The way I look at it is this. It was an unknown factor I had to solve and I solved it – years ago – and it's not much use to me now.

Mark It's not, eh?

Pete No.

Mark Well, I think you could do yourself a bit of good to give it another run.

Mark moves off. Pete follows.

Pete No. I don't think that's the answer to anything.

V

Virginia's place. Virginia tries on a white summer dress. Pete watches.

Pete Stay still. Go to the window.

She walks to the window, gazes at her reflection.

Like it?

Virginia Yes.

Pete Stay where you are. The sun's down your sides and on your neck. You look lovely.

Virginia It's beautiful. Thank you.

Pete It suits you.

Virginia I'll reserve it for special occasions.

Pete Summer's the occasion for that dress. I want to see you walk in the air.

Virginia In the sun.

Pete Yes. It was worth the doing.

Virginia Where have you been?

Pete I went down to the embankment. To watch the boats go by. A bit of quiet. It's like a monkey's tea party in that office.

Virginia The girls?

Pete Yes.

Virginia What do they do?

Pete I never look. Probably tickling each other in the vernacular. I keep well out of it.

Virginia Do they let you?

Pete They don't come near me. They know I'd cut 'em into tripes.

Virginia Was it hot today?

Pete Hot? I was mummified. The sea air did me good. Nice to watch the muck float.

Virginia I've been sitting here . . .
Did you enjoy making the dress?

Pete I moved a pawn with every stitch. It came off. Would you like me to make you a petticoat?

Virginia Yes please.

Pete I'll do that. I like you today.

He turns her to him and kisses her.

You know what? (*Sitting down.*) In some ways you're more of a boy to me than a woman.

Virginia What do you mean?

Pete No, you're a woman all right. But I like the way you conserve your mental energy. I can learn a lot from that, myself. But what you are, you're a good pal to me. You're a true companion.

Virginia Really?

Pete Yes. You see, Mark, for instance, could never understand that. A woman is simply one thing to him and no more. He wants all his women to call him sir and salute him three times a day. Another thing that niggles me is I'm sure he rides barebacked most of the time and doesn't give it a thought.

Virginia But you like him, don't you?

Pete Like him? Of course I like him.

Virginia He's a listener.

Pete He's a diehard. That's what he is. He was trying to convince me the other day that the answer to my problems was to go to bed with you more often.

Virginia Mark?

Pete Yes.

Virginia But how does he know? I mean, how does he know anything? About us?

Pete I don't know. I probably mentioned it to him.

Virginia You mean you told him we don't make love very often?

Pete Yes.

Virginia Oh.

Pete Why? Do you mind?

Virginia No.

Pete It's hardly anything to be ashamed of.

Virginia Yes, but why don't we write out a joint statement and send it to him?

Pete There's no need to do that.

Virginia To ease his mind.

Pete I don't think he's uncommonly disturbed about our problems.

Virginia He may be. He may be extremely concerned. Of course, I could always send him a poison pen letter, telling him to mind his own bloody business.

Pete Hey, wait a minute.

Virginia Do we actually need his technical hints?

Pete Now hold on. First of all, you're talking about a friend of mine. Secondly, what he said you've heard entirely out of context, and thirdly, let's face it, there may be a grain of truth in it.

Virginia Oh?

Pete Yes, but you have to weigh that grain of truth against the case in hand. After all, a fuck is a fuck but it doesn't take place in a vacuum. The context is concrete.

Virginia So's the fuck.

Pete That's beside the point.

VI

Len, at home, alone.

Len There is the table. That is a table. There is the chair. There is the table. That is a bowl of fruit. There is the tablecloth. There are the curtains. There is no woman in this room. This is a room. There is the wallpaper, on the walls. There are six walls. Eight walls. An octagon. This room is an octagon, with no woman and one cat. Above the fireplace is a mirror. There are my shoes, on my feet. There is no wind. It is neither night nor morning. This room moves. The room is moving. It has moved. It has reached – a dead halt. There is no enemy. There is no web. All's clear and abundant. All is ordered, in its place, no error has been made, here is my arrangement, I have my allies, I have my objects, I have my carpet, I have my land, this is a kingdom, there is no betrayal, there is no trust, they make no hole in my side.

They make a hole in my side.

A knock at the door. Len hunts for his glasses. Finally finds them in the top pocket of his jacket. He puts them on, walks to the front door and opens it. Mark enters.

Mark What were you doing? A war dance? I could see your shadow bobbing up and down.

Len How could you see my shadow?

Mark Through the letterbox.

Len What's this, a suit? Where's your carnation?

Mark What do you think of it?

Len fingers the lapels.

Len It's not a schmutta.

Mark It's got a zip at the hips.

Len A zip at the hips? What for?

Mark Instead of a buckle. It's neat.

Len Neat? I should say it's neat.

Mark No turn-ups.

Len I can see that. Why didn't you have turn-ups?

Mark It's smarter without turn-ups.

Len Of course it's smarter without turn-ups.

Mark I didn't want it double-breasted.

Len Double-breasted? Of course you couldn't have it double-breasted.

Mark What do you think of the cloth?

Len The cloth? What a piece of cloth. What a piece of cloth. What a piece of cloth. What a piece of cloth. What a piece of cloth.

Mark You like the cloth?

Len WHAT A PIECE OF CLOTH!

Len sits and groans. Mark combs his hair.

Mark Do you know where I've just been?

Len Where?

Mark Earls Court.

Len Uuuuhh!

Mark What's the matter with Earls Court?

Len It's a mortuary without a corpse. How did you get back, all-night bus?

Mark Of course.

Len Which one?

Mark A 297 to Fleet Street. A 296 from there.

Len I can get you from Notting Hill Gate to here in an hour to the minute.

Mark You can get *me*?

Len Any time of the night. Say you're at Notting Hill Gate at 1.52, no, it's Shepherds Bush at 1.52, say you're at Notting Hill Gate at 1.56 or 1.57, you can catch a 289 which gets to Marble Arch about 2.05, or 6, about

2.06, and there, before you know where you are, you can pick up a 291 or 294, coming from the Edgware Road, gets to Marble Arch about 2.07. What did I say? That's right. That's it. You catch that to the Aldwych, gets there about 2.15 or 14 and at 2.16 you can pick up the 296 from Waterloo, takes you all the way to Hackney. If it's after three o'clock you can do the whole lot on a workman's ticket.

Mark Thanks very much. What are you doing at Notting Hill Gate?

Len Notting Hill Gate? That was for your benefit. I never go anywhere near Notting Hill Gate.

Mark scratches himself in the groin and stretches his legs.

Mark What were you doing, when I knocked on your door?

Len Doing? Thinking.

Mark What about?

Len Nothing. It was about nothing. This room. Nothing.

Mark What's the matter with this room?

Len What's the matter with it? It doesn't exist! What are you doing here? What do you want here?

Mark I thought you might give me a piece of bread and honey.

Len I'll tell you something. As you're here . . . (*Fetching bread and honey.*) I know the nothing. The waste and the dead air. But for Pete, even the nothing is something positive. Pete's nothing eats away, it's voracious, it's a malignant growth. But, can't you see, he fights back, he grapples to the death with it. He's a fighter. My nothing doesn't bother to act in such a way. It licks its paws while I shrink. It's a true nothing, a paralysis.

Mark Monkeynuts.

Len Why do you say that?

Mark Catpiss.

Len All right, all right. If you believe that, I'll ask you another question.

Mark Ask.

Len What have you got against Jesus Christ?

Mark That's a fast yorker.

Len Can you play it?

Mark Which firm does he work for?

Len He's a freelance.

Mark Oh yes, he runs a book down at the dogs, doesn't he?

Len He runs a book all right.

Mark That's the bloke. Why? Has he put you on to any good things lately?

Len He's given me a few hot tips, I can tell you that. (*Mark coughs.*) But Mark, you can do me a favour and don't spit. You don't have to spit. You must have manners, even if you've got nothing else.

Mark Listen, Len, all you've got to do is put up a notice: Spitting Prohibited. Who could argue with that?

Len Yes, that's a good idea. I'll do that.

Mark clears his throat, bangs his chest, and sniffs.

What's the matter with you? You're farting and belching all over the place.

Mark What?

Len You think I'm mistaken. (*Mark shrugs.*) But am I?

Mark Am you?

Len (*raking his hair*) You're too big for me. You and Pete. You eat me out of house and home. Did you know you two are a music-hall act? And just because you've put a penny in my slot you think I'll go on talking for ever! But you're wrong. I'm not dead, at all events. You could say I'm dead and alive at successive times . . . In, out, dead, alive. Some people would call it an interesting period.

Mark stares at him.

Mark I'll have to use a stop watch in a minute!

Len doubles up, guffawing.

Len What can I do? What, I ask you, can I do?

Mark You should wear a hat.

Len Grow a moustache.

Mark Get a wheelchair.

Len False nose can work wonders.

Mark What else have you got here? Have you got any gherkins?

Len I slave my guts out. And I get nothing out of it! (*As he goes to the kitchen.*) Why can't you light a cigarette and look normal?

Exit Len.

VII

Pete and Virginia in bed. They kiss.

Pete You don't close your eyes.

Virginia No.

Pete Why not?

Virginia I want to see you.

Pete Why?

Virginia Because I love you.

Pete Yes, so do I. (*Pause.*) Listen. Do you believe I love you?

Virginia Do you?

Pete Do you believe it?

Virginia No.

Pete You're wrong. I love you. In some ways I'm very backward. But I'm becoming less ignorant.

Virginia Ignorant?

Pete I think I'm learning to love you.

Virginia How?

Pete Perhaps you're teaching me. Who else could?

Virginia Me?

Pete Who else?

She sits up.

Virginia The other day you told me I was like a boy to you.

Pete I said in some ways. All this, I see now, has been happening in me for some time, and I haven't been sufficiently aware of it. Or perhaps I was reluctant to trust it. I've been learning to love you for some time.

Virginia is silent.

Virginia Are you sure?

Pete No. But I want to be. I want you to help me prove it.

Virginia Yes.

Pete We can do it. I'm sure of that. Hey.

Virginia Yes?

Pete I'm going to stay here tonight.

Virginia You are?

Pete Yes.

Virginia I can't remember when you last did that.

Pete Well, there you are.

Virginia Here I am and here you are. Would you like to dance with me?

Pete What do you mean? Now?

Virginia Yes.

Pete Not at the moment, eh?

Virginia All right.

Pete Let's have some wine.

He stands up, walks to the table and pours two glasses of wine.

Virginia You're very slim, very tight.

Pete Cheers. (*He stands at the window, looking out.*) There's no wind.

Virginia Len once said that to me.

Pete What?

Virginia He just looked at me and he said, there's no wind.

Pete Ah, Len. I'm going to see him tomorrow night.

He bends his head and looks up at the sky.

All quiet up there, anyway.

Virginia Sounds very grave.

Pete What does?

Virginia Going to see Len tomorrow night.

Pete No. Why?

He sits down by her.

Did I ever tell you what my bugbear was when I used to knock about with Mark – in the days I was one of the boys? Armourplated women. It's one stage less difficult than making love to a crowbar. I remember once a suspender snapped. We were sitting on a tombstone in Hackney graveyard. I was caught between the buckle and the other machinery. I nearly had a penis stricture . . . She was a nurse, that one. Fully qualified.

Virginia Did you and Mark always go about together, then?

Pete Yes. Shift work.

He climbs into bed and holds her in his arms.

Virginia This is good for me.

Pete For me too.

Virginia It's not right for a schoolteacher to sleep alone all the time.

VIII

Len at his table, studying. He jots a note.

Len What are they doing, on their journeys to the street corners? Pete cannot hear the backchat, the cross-talk. He is listening to himself. Now Mark, who combs his hair in mirrors. He sings the song of Mark to the cocked glass. He sees himself and smiles . . . I am prepared to wait. I do not want to stop waiting. The end of this vigil is the beginning of nothing.

A knock at the door. Len, on tiptoe, lets in Pete.

'Noble my Lord, most fortunately welcome.' But whatever you do, don't wake the cat up.

Pete Do me a favour.

Len You don't understand. Today I was playing Bach to that cat. I was trying a sonata for unaccompanied violin. Can't you see? He deserves a rest.

Pete That cat has ceased to be the animal he was. Look at him. He's become a semiquaver.

Len You can't lay everything at Bach's door.

Pete Why not? He rules this house with a rod of iron. What do you call him?

Len Solomon.

Pete Tell me something, who was Bach?

Len Who was he? You can't ask me a question like that!

Pete You must know something about him. What was he up to?

Len fetches wine.

Len Ask someone else. I can't tell you. It's out of the question. I can't speak about him.

Pete No?

Len Bach? It's simple. The point about Bach – the point about Bach – the point about Bach is that – give me a chance – is that –

He sits on the table and stands hurriedly, slapping the seat of his trousers.

Ugh! Ugh! Ugh!

Pete Use a rag.

Len Ugh!

Pete Turn round. There's nothing there.

Len I'm wet through.

Pete You were talking about Bach.

Len Thirty-nine-and-six five years ago. (*Taking off his trousers.*)

Pete Why don't you stand on your head next? What about, for Christsake get on with it, bloody Bach?

Len Bach? It's simple. Look at Beethoven.

Pete What do you mean?

Len Beethoven is always Beethoven. Bach is like cold or heat or water or flame. He is Bach but he's not Bach. There's no comparison.

Pete Wait a minute –

Len Bach is not concerned with murder, nature, massacre, earthquake, famine, plague, rebellion or the other one. He is not concerned with big things as such.

Pete Huh?

Len (*pulling on his trousers*) They tell me, Pete, that a warm and generous woman makes all else pale into insignificance. Even Shakespeare becomes a few well chosen words. But Bach could never become, for me, a few well chosen notes. That's all I've got to say about Bach. There you are. You shouldn't have asked me.

Pete What about a cup of cocoa?

Len Cocoa?

Pete Yes, we'll drink a toast.

Len All right. All right. I don't mind doing that.

Pete My face is a death's head. (*Looking in mirror.*)

Len (*off*) You're quite right.

Pete This is a very solid table.

Len (*off*) I've got a few bagels.

Pete No thanks. How long have you had this table?

Len It's a family heirloom.

Pete Yes, I'd like a good table and a good chair. Solid stuff. I'd put them in a boat. Sail it down the river. A houseboat. You could sit in the cabin and look out at the water.

Len (*off*) Who'd be steering?

Pete You could park it. There's not a soul in sight. Sun all shapes and sizes. There ahead, the calmest patch of water you've ever seen.

Len (*returning*) Here's your cocoa.

Pete How's Mark?

Len Fine.

Pete What does he have to say for himself?

Len He said he wouldn't spit last night.

Pete I'm glad to hear it.

Len I'm glad to be able to say it.

Pete What's he got to spit about?

Len Well, he likes a good spit sometimes. He said something else, though, that I'm sure you'll appreciate.

Pete What's that?

Len He was talking about Dean Swift, you see, and he said he ended up eating his own shit and left his money to lunatic asylums. Have you seen Pete lately? Straight off. What do you think of that?

Pete laughs.

Pete That's very amusing.

Len Amusing! I should say it is.

Pete Yes, he's a strange chap is Mark. I sometimes think he's a man of weeds. And yet I don't know. He surprises me, that bloke, now and again, for the good, I mean. But often I wonder about him. I sometimes think he's just playing a game. But what game?

Pause.

Well, how are you, Len? How's things?

Len Huh. I'm supper for the crows. I'm a non-participator.

Pete Go home. You? You're just a Charley Hunt.

Len That too.

Pete You need to be more elastic.

Len Elastic? Elastic, you're quite right. Elastic!

Pete Here, I'll tell you a dream I had last night, if you like, to cheer you up.

Len All right.

Pete I didn't expect to dream last night.

Len What was it?

Pete It was very straightforward. I was with Virginia in a tube station, on the platform. People were rushing about. There was some sort of panic. When I looked round, I saw everyone's faces were peeling, blotched, blistered. People were screaming, booming down the tunnels. There was a firebell clanging. When I looked at Ginny, I saw that her face was coming off in slabs too. Like plaster. Black scabs and stains. The skin was dropping off like lumps of catsmeat. I could hear it sizzling on the electric rails. I pulled her by the arm to get her out of there, she wouldn't budge, she just stood there, with half a face, staring at me. I screamed at her to come away, but she still wouldn't move. Then I suddenly thought – Christ, what's my face like? Is that what she's staring at? Is that rotting too?

Len gasps.

One for the black book, eh?

Len covers his eyes with his hands.

Doesn't matter about that. Watch this. See how many I can do?

Len What?

Pete Keep a count.

Pete lies on the floor and begins to propel himself up and down on his forearms.

How many?

Len Fifteen.

Pete continues.

Twenty.

Pete Uh.

Len Twenty-five.

Pete Uh.

Len Twenty-nine.

Pete Enough.

He relaxes and grins, sitting on the floor.

Not bad, eh?

Len What are you made of? It's beyond me.

Pete Give me a week and I'll do thirty-five.

IX

Mark's room. Pete and Mark playing chess. Neither looks at Len.

Len Eh . . . The dwarfs are back on the job. (*Pause.*) I said the dwarfs are back on the job.

Mark The what?

Len The dwarfs.

Mark Oh yes?

Len Oh yes. They've been waiting for a smoke signal, you see. I've just sent up the smoke signal.

Pause.

Mark You've just sent it up, have you?

Len Yes. I've called them in on the job. They've taken up their positions. Haven't you noticed?

Pete I haven't noticed. Have you noticed?

Mark chuckles.

Len But I'll tell you one thing. They don't stop work until the job in hand is finished, one way or another. They never run out on a job. Oh no. They're true professionals. Real professionals.

Pete Listen. Can't you see we're trying to play chess?

Pause.

Len I've called them in to keep an eye on you two, you see. They're going to keep a very close eye on you. So am I . . . We can't see this particular assignment lasting into the winter. The game'll be up by then.

Mark I think I've got you knackered, Pete.

Pete Do you?

Pete concedes defeat. He stands.

See you, Mark.

Pete exits.

Mark Why don't you leave Pete alone?

Len Leave him alone?

Mark Why don't you give it a rest? He doesn't do you any good. I'm the only one who can get on with him.

Len You?

Mark Yes. You've got to have a certain kind of – something – to get on with him. Anyway, I've got it and at the moment you haven't.

Len You get on with him?

Mark He doesn't take any liberties with me. He does with you.

Len What makes you think he takes liberties with me?

Mark Do what you bloody well like.

Len You mean come over to your side.

Mark What do you mean?

Silence.

X

Hackney Downs. Pete, Mark and Len sitting outside. Evening.

Pete (*sings*) 'Come away, come away, death, and in sad cypress let me be laid . . .' I'll tell you what, thinking got me into this and thinking's got to get me out. You know what I want? An efficient idea. One that'll work. Something I can pin my money on. I'm willing to gamble. I gambled when I went to work in the City. I want to fight them on their own ground! The time has come to act. Of course, some people are efficient ideas in themselves. You might be an efficient idea yourself, Mark. You can never tell.

Mark I should think they're very few and far between, efficient ideas.

Len Like a nutcracker. You press the cracker and the cracker cracks the nut. There's no waste of energy. It's an exact process and an efficient one.

Pete No, you're wrong. There is waste. When you press the cracker with the proper purchase the nut cracks, but at the same time the hinge of the cracker gives out a friction, a heat, which is incidental. It's exactly the same, after all, with a work of art. Every particle of a work of art should crack a nut, or help form a pressure that'll crack the final nut. Only then can you speak of utterance, and only then can you speak of achievement.

Len What about the sun and moon? Isn't there something ambiguous about the sun and moon?

Pete Of course there's nothing against a geezer constructing his own idea. But he's got to be able to determine to what the idea is relevant. It's a matter of considering what world you're relating it to.

Mark Well, we can't make any mistake about that.

Pete I don't know. I don't know that we quite agree on that point, Mark. I mean what it comes down to is what world, exactly, are you talking about?

Mark I know what world you're talking about. The bus ticket world.

Pete All right. You have tuppence in your pocket and you pay your fare. But you actually regard the conveyance as your divine right. The way you pay your tuppence you don't really pay it at all. You're getting a free ride.

Mark I'm a liability on the world's bank balance.

Pete You're not only a liability, you're a bloody hallucination. Sometimes I can't believe you exist at all.

Mark But where you do believe I exist, is as a parasite.

Pete Not exactly.

Mark A parasite. But it's inaccurate. I follow my itch, that's all.

Pete That's the point. What I'm accusing you of is operating on life and not in it.

Mark If I'm a ponce, I'm my own ponce. I live and I operate in my own life.

Pete Your danger, Mark, is that you might become nothing but an attitude.

Mark Not while I've still got balls, mate.

Pete They won't save you. They might drop off.

Mark I keep them well oiled.

Pete Ah, there may be some truth in that. I told you, you might be an efficient idea.

Len . . . They've gone on a picnic.

Mark Who?

Len The dwarfs.

Pete Oh Christ.

Len They've left me to sweep the yard, to keep the place in order. It's a bloody liberty. I'm not a skivvy, they don't pay me, I pay them!

Mark Why don't you settle down?

Len Oh, don't worry, it's basically a happy relationship. I trust them. I like watching them. Always squatting and bending, dipping their wicks in the custard.

Mark Listen. It's about time I told you people something else – for your own good.

Pete What?

Mark Did you know I was born circumcised?

Pete What!

Mark The geezer came along with the carving knife to do the necessary and nearly dropped down dead with the shock. They had to give him a double brandy on the house. He thought I was the Messiah.

Len Well, own up. Are you?

Virginia joins them, carrying a book.

Pete Well, how's Marie?

Virginia She's very well.

Mark Marie Saxon? What's she doing now?

Pete She spends most of her time in Soho. Prancing about with all and sundry.

Mark She was mad about me in the old days.

Pete She isn't the one that you banged round the earhole once?

Mark No. That was Rita.

Pete Oh yes. Rita.

Len What was that?

Pete She was leading him up the garden or something, so he knocked her teeth in.

Mark Not quite, but she asked for it, anyway. So Marie's not in love with me any more, eh?

Pete Love? She's flogging her whatsit to bellboys and pisshounds.

Mark What's the book, Virginia?

Virginia *Hamlet*.

Pete *Hamlet?*

Mark What's it like?

Virginia Do you know, it's odd, but I suddenly can't find any virtue in the man.

Mark Really?

Virginia No.

Mark Why?

Virginia No, no, I – after all, what is he? What is he but vicious, maudlin, spiteful, and sensitive to nothing but his own headaches? I find him completely unprepossessing.

She sits back.

Mark (*laughing*) Well, it's a point of view.

Pete You're quite wrong, of course.

Virginia I don't know. What does he do but talk and talk, and now again stick a knife into someone. I mean a sword.

Pete I find this rather amusing. But we won't go into it.

Len (*standing*) I've got to go.

Pete Yes, we'll adjourn.

Mark All-night shift?

Len Yes. There's my bus.

Pete Be seeing you.

Len exits, running.

You can see yourself home, Ginny? I think I'll go straight back.

Virginia Of course.

Mark Shall I see you home?

Virginia No, no, it's quite all right.

Pete My bus. See you. Ta-ta Mark.

He walks away.

Virginia Well, I'd better be off.

Mark watches her lips move.

Mark I can easily –

Virginia No, it's all right, Mark. It's only five minutes.

Mark How are you?

Virginia Fine.

Mark Uh-huh.

Virginia Well, I'd better be going. I'll be seeing you.

Mark Yes.

Virginia Cheerio.

Mark Goodnight.

Virginia Goodnight.

XI

Pete in a call-box.

Pete Ginny?
Are you in?
All right. I'm coming round now.
I'll be there in half an hour.
Don't go out.

XII

Pete enters Virginia's flat. Virginia is in her bathrobe.

Virginia I've just had a bath.

Pete What for?

Virginia What?

He takes off his jacket and tie and wipes his face.

Did you have a bad day?

Pete What do you mean, bad day?

Virginia Bad day. Bad day.

Pete Why have you had a bath?

Virginia It's hot.

He turns and looks at Virginia, her bathrobe open.

Look how pink my nipples are. Like a virgin.

Pete Will you do that thing up?

Virginia Why?

Pete Do you mind doing it up?

She ties the cord and sits.

Who was round here this afternoon?

Virginia How do you know anyone was here?

Pete The cups, the cups. Who was it?

Virginia My friend Marie Saxon.

Pete What did she want?

Virginia A cup of tea.

Pete What did she want?

Virginia Christ. She didn't want anything.

Pete She's a prostitute.

Virginia No she's not.

Pete She's a scrubber.

Virginia smoothes her hair.

Did you have your bath while she was here?

Virginia Why?

Pete Did she soap your armpits?

Virginia Christ.

Pete Will you stop saying that?

Virginia No. I don't know what to say.

Pete Why say anything?

Virginia Ah.

Pete (*shouting*) And for God's sake keep that robe done up! I don't want to see the hair on your crutch. What do you think I am?

She closes her robe.

Virginia I don't know what I think you are.

Pete I know you don't. I'm damn sure you don't. It's about time you stopped continually powdering your fanny and opened your eyes, mate. Why, for instance, don't you go and put some clothes on now? Don't you realise that someone might knock on that door and that you've got no right to open it like that?

Virginia You could open it.

Virginia picks up a Picture Post *magazine and leafs through it.*

Pete You're being very disappointing, Virginia. You're behaving like any other little tart who must show herself off or cease to exist.

Virginia I've just had a bath.

Pete It's normal to dress after a bath.

Virginia Oh for God's sake!

Pete So if there's a knock at the door, you'll go to it like that?

Virginia I don't expect anyone.

Pete Don't be stupid. Anyone's liable to turn up. A man may come to examine the meters.

Virginia He only comes in the mornings.

Pete How can you be sure?

Virginia He's at home. Mowing the garden.

Pete Quite honestly, you're nothing but a dead weight. I know there are men who would be glad to accept you as you are. We know their requirements. Why don't you get Marie Saxon to introduce you to some motorcyclists, or all-in wrestlers?

Virginia Yes, I'll think about that.

Pete What else do you think about, Virginia?

Virginia Nothing else.

Pete I wonder what you and Marie Saxon discuss?

Virginia Only one thing. Jockstraps.

Pete If you're falling into that error, I'm disappointed, to be quite frank. I've told you before –

Virginia Pete! What do you want? What do you want me to do? What have I done? Please! What have I done? Tell me.

He looks down at her.

Pete Why did you say that thing about Hamlet last night?

Virginia What thing?

Pete About Hamlet. Why did you say it? Why do you say these things? Do you know they're extremely stupid? It made me look very foolish. Did you think Mark would be impressed? You don't know anything about Hamlet, Ginny. But you lug the book about with you like a pissy fifth-former, and parade these stupidities. In other less charitable company you would have had your balls chopped off. But what I don't understand is your motive. Were you deliberately trying to make me look like a fool? It was morally indefensible and morally objectionable. Did you think you would be excused because you were a woman? I'm willing to help you all

I can in such matters, but such an action on your part almost amounts to a stab in the back. What you must do is develop a sense of proportion, of judgement. You have the faculties but you seem reluctant to use them. Why are you crying? I tell you, you have the faculties. It's just a matter of bringing them into focus, of sharpening them. You've no need to cry. I know you've understood me. All that happened was that your artistic sensibility, your sense of proportion, went astray. I admire these qualities in you, Ginny, I always have done, I merely felt bound to point out –

Virginia I'm sorry. I'm sorry. I won't do it again.

Pete No. (*Sitting on the chair arm, holding her to his chest.*) It's all right. It's all right.

Virginia I'm sorry, I'm sorry.

Pete No. It's all right. It's all right.

XIII

Len at home, writing.

Len No sooner do they leave, these dwarfs, than in come the rats. When they return from their picnics I tell them I've had a clearance. They don't know the difference. They yawn, they show the blood stuck between their teeth, they play their scratching game, they tongue their chops, they make monsters of their innocent catch, they gorge. What about the job in hand? After all my devotion. What about the rats I saved for you, what about the ratsteak I tried all ways to please you? They don't touch it, they're hiding it till the time I can no longer stand upright and I fall, they'll bring it out then, grimed then, green, varnished, rigid, and eat it as a victory dish.

XIV

At Mark's. Virginia, Pete, Mark and Len drinking tea.

Mark Very good tea that, Virginia.

Virginia Good.

Len Look here, I'll tell you something for nothing. I went into the washroom at work the other day and the stationmaster, the big boss, the king of the castle, was bending over a basin washing his hands, immaculately dressed. I couldn't believe my eyes. I stood there looking at him and I had a terrible temptation to kick him straight up the arse.

Mark Did you?

Len No. Do you know why? Can't you see why? If I'd have kicked him there and then and knocked him through the mirror, don't you know what he would have done? He'd have turned round and said, I'm most awfully sorry, wiped his hands, and gone out. Like God. It's exactly what God would do. It stands to reason.

Pete Yes. It's all very well, but you've got to keep a firm grip on your inclinations in these places. You've got to be armourplated. There's a lot I could do and say if I behaved like a man and lost my temper. But what's the point? I'd rather cut my throat than bandy words with the kind of guttersnipe I run into.

Virginia takes the glasses into the kitchen.

Len Croquet weather, it's croquet weather.

Mark The duke's a long time coming, said the duchess, stirring the tea with her other hand.

Pete Yes, but there's no real weather in London. London's an overall condition. Come on, Weinblatt. Do your best and put a frown on. I'm getting on to metaphysics.

Virginia comes back into the room and sits.

Mark I've discovered an art . . . to find the mind's construction in the arse.

Len That's a lovely dress, Virginia.

Virginia Haven't you seen it before?

Len Have I?

Virginia Pete made it.

Pete Yes, it's a good fit, that dress.

Len bends down and fingers the dress.

Len That's a very fair piece of material.

Mark Wholesale or retail?

Pete Wholesale. I know a bloke.

Len How much are you retail, then?

Virginia I'm not in season.

Pete and Mark light cigarettes.

Pete When are you going to do a job of work, Mark?

Mark Not for some time yet.

Pete Where do you get your pocket money?

Mark I've got a duchess in Hanover Square.

Virginia Old or young?

Mark She's bedridden.

Pete I don't doubt it.

Mark As a matter of fact, that is my earnest ambition.

Pete Don't kid yourself. You wouldn't be any good as a gigolo. A gigolo has to be faithful and satisfied with his lot. You'd be running after the kitchen maid, too.

Mark You've got something there.

Pete Be frank. Have you ever done an honest day's work in your life?

Mark When I'm working I'm nothing but a slave. A slave. Go on the stage yourself. Get a bucketful.

Pete No thanks.

Mark Why not? They'd lap you up.

Pete I'd die in a week. Quite frankly, when I think of the English dramatic heritage and then look around me at the crowd of poofs and ponces that support it I feel like throwing in the sponge.

Len shifts.

Len I've decided to go over to Paris next week.

Pete Paris? What for?

Len How can I tell you what for?

Mark Alone?

Len No. With a bloke at Euston. An Austrian.

Pete But what do you want to go to Paris for?

Virginia Why shouldn't he?

Pete You don't understand, Ginny. We've got Len's interests at heart. Haven't we, Len?

Len I'll take a return ticket. I might return within the hour. Who knows?

Mark Well, drop us a card.

Virginia stands, smoothing her dress.

Virginia I think I'll go for a walk in the garden.

Mark I'll come with you. Show you the lilac.

Len looks up.

Len Come with me?

Mark Not you.

Pete (*to Len*) It doesn't altogether ring true, Paris.

Mark and Virginia walk in the garden, and stand under the arch of a lilac tree.

Virginia I like this tree.

Mark Mind. Spider's web.

Virginia I didn't see it.

Mark That is a beautiful dress.

Virginia Yes.

Mark A man of many talents.

She plucks a leaf and presses it to her mouth.

Virginia Yes.

Mark How's school?

Virginia Fine.

Mark Do you still like the kids?

Virginia Yes, of course.

Mark And they like you?

Virginia I think so.

Mark Your arms are very brown.

Virginia We went into the country the other day. The kids and me. We went to Kent.

Mark Yes?

Virginia Mmn.

Mark Well, how's Marie Saxon?

Virginia She said to tell you she's managed to forget you.

Mark Sweet.

Virginia She said it was a hard job, but her heart has healed.

Mark What a shame

Virginia tears the leaf across, along the spine.

Virginia What do you do with yourself?

Mark Depends which way the wind's blowing.

Virginia Which way has it been blowing?

Mark I can't really remember. What about you?

Virginia Me?

Mark Yes.

Virginia In the pink. Let's go in.

They walk back. Inside:

Pete (*to Len*) What I mean is, Shakespeare didn't need to go further than his own front door.

Len But if someone had given him a ticket, would he have said no?

Pete No, I suppose not.

Len They may drive me out. They may not even let me in.

Mark What about a stroll?

Pete Yes. Good idea.

They all leave.

XV

They cross a road towards Hackney Downs.

Pete Very interesting book this, Len. About surgery in Elizabethan times. Do you know a woman once gave birth to six puppies?

Len No!

Mark (*glancing at newspaper*) Hutton's made a century against Essex.

Len He can't do anything right these days, can he?

Mark throws his newspaper away.

(*to Pete*) How did she manage it?

Pete (*screams*) For Jesus Christ's fucking sake! (*Hurling his books at Virginia's feet.*) Will you stop walking between those fucking paving stones? You're driving me mad!

Virginia Bastard! What do you mean? Bastard!

Pete I'll kill you, you fucking bitch, if you don't stop it!

Silence. Virginia walks slowly on. Pete picks up the books.

Well, if I don't see you before you go, Len, look after yourself in Paris.

Len I'll probably see you before I go.

Pete Yes. (*to Mark*) I'll be seeing you.

Mark Yes.

Pete catches up with Virginia. Len and Mark watch them. Virginia crouches in Pete's arms.

Len (*to Mark*) Are you coming?

They leave, Pete and Virginia one way, Len and Mark another.

Interval.

Act Two

XVI

Pete walks by the River Lea. Night.
  Sound of water. Shunting engine in the distance. Far off, an owl.
  Pete stops, murmurs to himself.

Pete 'Twas the melancholy bird,
 The owl, that screamed so.'

> *He moves on. Feet on gravel as he reaches the canal lock. He picks up a heavy stone, throws it. A dull splash.*
>   *Pete lowers himself, gripping a railing. Leans over the water.*
>   *Lies face down. Forces his head under water.*
>   *Long pause.*
>   *He jerks back, retching and gasping for air.*
>   *Slowly stands. Moves away.*

XVII

Pete's place. A council flat.
  Pete sitting alone.
  The door opens. Len joins him.

Len Pete?

Pause.

Pete (*smiling*) The emissary.

Len What do you mean?

Pete That's another question. I'm talking about yachts. They're as clean as a whistle. They have balance and proportion. They're a logical unit. That's the only thing to look for in this world. Logic. Logic in a drainpipe. Logic in a leaf.

Virginia has put on lipstick and gone out with a girlfriend. I have made my way home from the canal. You've stepped over the mat, into this room.

I won't abolish you. To say I have a screw loose would not be accurate. On the contrary, my screws are so tight they grind against each other from each side of my cranium. There is no need for you to pray. If you slip onto your knees and pray I shall be mortally offended. It would be a prayer for the dead. Love is easy in the nursery. The gas chamber, I won't deny it, is a ripe and purposive unit. I look into my garden and see walking blasphemies. A blasphemy is a terrible thing. They cut the throat of a child over the body of a naked woman. The blood runs down her back, the blood runs between the cheeks of her arse. In my sight the world commits sacrilege. The whole matter must be turned over to God and he can carry the can back. Let it never be said God is unreasonable. The world is vanity. The world is impertinent. I must cease to belong . . . What do you want?

Len Nothing.

Pete begins to raise himself from the chair.

What do you want?

Pete I want a glass of water.

Len I'll get it.

Pete Thanks.

Len goes, returns. Pete takes the glass and drinks.

Thanks.

Len sits. Pete licks his lips.

What was your idea in coming here?

Len I thought I'd pop in.

Pete closes his eyes.

Pete What time is it?

Len Three-ish.

Pete I am ill.

Len Yes.

Pete I wonder if you know what I lack?

Len frowns and bends his head.

Len I don't know.

Pete I lack guts.

Len I wouldn't say that.

Pete Yes. I lack guts.

Len Do you?

Pete You mustn't think that I don't know what you and Mark are. I do. I recognise you both.

Len What are we?

Pete I take it you are my friends.

Len grimaces and clips his palm under his jaw.

Len Yes.

Pete Why don't you ask me if I recognise Virginia?

Len Why should I ask you that?

Pete If you want to know another thing, I'll tell you. Because I lack guts, I commit spite. Do you know what that makes me?

Len It makes you Shammes to the Pope of China.

Pete Very true.

Len What else?

Pete That could be it, I admit. Have you ever met the Pope of China?

Len Yes.

Pete What's he like?

Len He's like you.

Pete No, I'm his Shammes.

Len You're also the Pope of China.

Pete No. That's where you're wrong. (*He stands.*) Air.

Len Where are you going?

Pete Outside.

They move out to the balcony. Len rubs his eyes.

Len My eyes are very bad. Now I've taken off my glasses, I can see.

Pete That's reasonable.

Len Isn't that the moon up there? It must be late. Can you see the lights there, on the roads? All that. They have that sound. I can see the moon where I stand. It's all right. The globe's turning. Can you hear the moon? Eh? And these lights? We're making the light. Can you hear the moon, through the sound? It is in us.

XVIII

Mark's place. Mark, Pete, Len and Virginia in animated conversation.

Mark The world's got nothing on me. Where's the bother?

Len You're a marked man.

Mark Possibly. Marked but indifferent.

Pete Would you be indifferent to the torturing wheel?

Mark Oh no.

Virginia So you're not indifferent to everything?

Mark All I'm trying to say is that everything's a calamity. There are items within the fact of that fact that I am unable to accept. But I accept that I can't accept them. In other words I carry on merrily.

Pete It does me good to hear it.

Len Your uncle must have been Chief Rabbi.

Mark Why?

Len Why? You're steeped in Talmudic evasion!

Mark What did the Talmud ever evade?

Len How do I know? I've never read it, as such.

Pete As such, yes.

Len You're very chirpy tonight.

Virginia Do you enjoy life?

Mark Up to the neck.

Len You're looking very well today, Ginny.

Virginia I'm feeling it.

Mark Every time.

Pete Make me a willow whatsaname at your gate.

Mark And call upon my howdoyoudo within the house.

Pete That's it.

Mark What does she say to that?

Virginia Olivia?

Mark Yes.

Virginia You might do much . . . I'll take the cups.

She collects the cups and takes them into the kitchen.

Mark (*following her*) I'll wipe them up.

Pete When are you off, Len?

Len Tomorrow.

Pete Look. Here's a couple of quid. Might come in handy.

Len No, that's all right.

Pete Take it.

Len All right. Thanks.

Mark leans by the kitchen door.

Mark Lovely evening.

Virginia (*off*) It is.

Mark Where's the wiper?

Virginia (*off*) Let me do it. You go back.

Mark Sure?

Virginia (*off*) Yes.

Mark re-joins Len and Pete.

Pete I wouldn't mind making a trip myself.

Len Why don't you?

Pete I will one day. But it'll be farther off.

Virginia walks into the garden, shivering. She covers her face. Pete follows her.

Virginia.

Pete walks across to the lilac arch.

What are you doing?

Virginia Watching it get dark.

He draws her back to him and presses her breasts.

Pete Ginny –

Virginia It's cold.

He turns her to him.

Pete Is it?

Virginia looks into his eyes.

Virginia Yes.

Inside:

Mark What are they up to out there? Should I tell them I possess the best bed in Hackney?

Len observes him.

Well, it's all in the way you tie your tie. (*Picks up a book.*) Thomas Aquinas. Never read a word of it. Am I better off or worse off?

Len Worse.

Mark sits.

You're straining at the leash.

Mark What leash?

Len I only know you're straining.

Mark You're off the mark.

Virginia and Pete return to the room.

Pete We're off.

Mark Uh-huh.

Virginia I watched the night arrive.

Mark Very nice too.

Len I can't do that.

Virginia Why not?

Len No. Impossible. I can't look at the sky.

Mark What's there to it? First it's day, then it's night.

Pete Mother Nature? I thought you were partial. (*To Len*) Well, watch yourself in Paris, Len.

Len I will.

Virginia Have a good time.

Len Thanks.

Pete Keep in touch.

Len I will.

Mark Be seeing you, Pete.

Pete Yes. Cheerio.

Virginia Cheerio.

Mark Cheerio.

Len Cheerio.

Pete and Virginia leave.

XIX

A pub. Pete and Mark, drinking.

Pete The point about Shakespeare (*thumping the table*) is that he didn't measure the man up against the idea and give you hot tips on the outcome.

Mark He wasn't a betting man.

Pete He laid bare, that's all. I'd defy any man who said he saw good and evil as abstractions. He didn't.

Mark Well?

Pete Leave Hamlet out of it, he's another story. Othello is jealous because of an excess of love. Macbeth's real trouble was he thought too much of his wife. Their feelings are in excess of the facts.

Mark Ah. So where are we now?

Pete Back where we started.

Mark Where's that?

Pete Back in the booze. Come to me when I'm sober.

Virginia appears, isolated in a pool of light.

Virginia Look. The moon and the black leaves. The bright day is done. He has managed to banish me. What he hoped and what he feared. I have taken the hint.

She turns away.

Pete Follow me. I am the way and the truth. I am the resurrection and the life.

Mark I believe you.

Pete It's gospel. When I was born they were waiting on the doorstep with a form for me to fill up. I said I'd accept the job on two conditions.

Mark What were they?

Pete First, that I was to have a free hand.

Mark What did they say to that?

Pete Wouldn't give me a straight answer.

Mark It's a carve-up. What was the second condition?

Pete I wanted a worthwhile Judas.

Mark Well?

Pete I haven't met anyone who was quite up to the mark. Give me your glass.

He goes to the bar. Virginia turns.

Virginia I shall throw my hand in. Scrub round it. Under stealth I lived, under stealth I'll leave. I am cold with the years of you.

Pete returns with beers.

Mark Eh, wait a minute, you must be the Holy Ghost.

Pete Up your Holy Ghost. (*They drink.*) Look here. I once thought I was a genius. I'm not. I'm a specimen. And another thing, while we're at it. I've said a few rude things about you in the past. And I don't take them back. But the truth's all things. Your faults don't make your virtues any less true.

Mark I haven't got any faults. I am composed of properties and characteristics. No moral blame attached. I have no faults.

Pete Now, now. You can't wash all the blackheads off your face with a statement like that. You might wash your face away. And what would a geezer like you do without a face?

Mark (*rising*) No bones broken.

Mark goes to the bar. Virginia turns.

Virginia You came to me in that garden. I told you I was cold. You knew what I said. I am a bat. I must not be a bat. I shall leave you.

The figure of Virginia fades. Mark returns from the bar with two double whiskies.

Pete Hallo, hallo.

Mark No holds barred.

Pete Well, who shall we toast?

Mark Let's toast Virginia.

Pete Right.

Mark In what fashion?

Pete Austerely. To Virginia.

Mark A textbook toast.

They raise glasses.

We must drink to Len sometime too.

Pete We can do that with the beer.

Mark Of course.

Pete We'll do this one first.

Mark Right.

Pete Okay.

Mark Wait a minute. We don't touch glasses?

Pete No. That's elaboration.

Mark That's true.

They raise glasses.

Pete To Virginia.

Mark To Virginia.

Pete Good whisky.

Mark Now for Len.

Pete Yes.

Mark We can't just say – to Len.

Pete To Weinblatt.

Mark Good enough.

They lift mugs.

To Weinblatt.

Pete To Weinblatt.

Mark I wonder what he's up to now.

Pete Probably sitting on top of the Arc de Triomphe, playing his recorder.

Mark I'm made of beer.

Pete Do you know there are beautiful women in this pub?

Mark Every time. Where's Virginia?

Pete She's at home.

Mark At home?

Pete At her home. I'm beginning to see things.

Mark See things? That's more than I am.

Pete I'm breaking through a question, through a false, mate, hypothesis.

Mark What are all these empty spaces?

Pete Shutting up shop. (*Rising.*) Up you get.

Mark Up, guards.

Pete Sit down or stand up.

Mark Dignity. Dignity!

Pete Come on!

Mark . . . You can't have too much of it.

They leave the pub. Mark stumbles. Pete catches him.

Pete Not a very efficient idea, this.

They put out their hands for a bus. The bus passes.

I've seen a ghost.

Mark What?

Pete Isn't that Len, just about to be run over?

Mark I don't believe it.

Len crosses the road. Pete and Mark approach him.

We don't want to know you.

Len (*smiling*) Merry Christmas.

Pete What have you done with Paris?

Len I left. I've only been back two days.

Mark Two days? What have you been doing?

Len Recuperating.

Pete You look as though the police of twelve continents are after you.

Len looks at them.

Mark Why did you leave?

Len Why did I leave? There's only one reason I left. I don't mind telling you. All right. I'll tell you.

Pete Well?

Len It was because of the cheese.

Pete The cheese?

Len The cheese. Stale Camembert cheese. It got me in the end. It all came out, I can tell you, in about twenty-eight goes. I couldn't stop shivering and I couldn't stop squatting. I'm all right now. I only go three times a day now. I can more or less regulate it. Once in the morning. A quick dash before lunch. Another quick dash after tea, and then I'm free to do what I want. The trouble with Camembert, you see, is that it doesn't die. In fact, it only begins to live when you swallow it. A German I got to know there used to take it to bed with him. He used to treat it brutally, that cheese. He would bite into it, really bite into it, and then concentrate. The sweat used to come out on his nose, but he always won. I hate to say it, but his piss stank worse than Old Testament Rabbis.

Pete You were in Paris for over a week. What else happened?

Len I can't remember. It's blotted everything else out. Whenever I think of Paris I just think of cheese.

Mark Come on. Why did you leave?

Len shakes his head and smiles.

Len It was that cheese, that's all. It was the cheese.

XX

Virginia's flat. She lets in Pete. He sits.

Pete Come here.

She sits by him on the sofa.

Virginia You work too hard.

Pete It's a working world.

He moves his feet onto the sofa arm.

How are you?

Virginia Fine.

Pete I popped into the library on the way home. For a solid hour I was looking through books on dogs, horses, anthropology, psychology, poetic works, oil-engines, how to be a lifeboatman and the inside story of a werewolf. Have you ever been a werewolf?

Virginia How would I know?

Pete A vampire bat?

Virginia I suppose you have.

Pete Me? I'm a clean-living customer. (*Pause.*) Len's back.

Virginia Len? That was quick.

Pete He's keeping something under his hat. Wouldn't say why, what, anything.

Virginia There's always this secrecy, this funny business.

Pete Funny business?

Virginia You never know why, what, anything.

Pete Oh, I don't know.

Virginia It's confusion. I don't believe –

Pete What?

Virginia I don't believe everyone need live like that.

Pete There's no need, no.

Virginia No.

Pete What are you going to buy me for my birthday?

Virginia Oh yes. What do you want?

Pete I want a book. I want a well-bound book that'll enlighten me. No long words. Big print.

Virginia All right.

Pete Eh, I was thinking. Do you ever dream about me?

Virginia You know I do.

Pete You should put a stop to that.

Virginia Should I?

She turns to the window.

Pete.

Pete Yes.

Virginia I want to ask you something.

Pete Mmn?

Virginia I need a rest.

Pete What?

Virginia I need a rest.

Pete A rest?

Virginia Yes.

Pete What do you mean?

Virginia I'm worn out.

He swings round to face her.

I need quiet. I need rest.

She is still.

Pete Rest from what?

Virginia From –

Pete From what?

Virginia Us.

Pete scratches the back of his head.

Pete Why? What's the matter?

Virginia I'm tired.

Pete Are you?

He walks over to the window and looks out.

Virginia Only for a little while.

Pete How long?

Virginia Just – about a fortnight.

Pete It's not all high voltage, all the time? Is it?

Virginia No.

Pete Well?

Virginia But I'm tired.

Pete What do you want to do with your fortnight?

Virginia Nothing.

Pete I can't see your face.

Virginia Can't you?

Pete Look at me.

Virginia I am.

Pete Can you see me?

Virginia Yes. You're white in the window.

Pete You're wearing my dress.

Virginia Yes.

Pete You didn't have to do that.

Virginia What do you mean?

He smiles.

Pete Okay, Ginny.

He looks out at the night.

Anyone would think we're in Eskimoland.

He turns.

Okay. You want a rest. Have one. I wish you luck.

Virginia Thank you.

Pete Two weeks. Don't worry. I won't fly in at your window like a vampire bat. It's not my bloodsucking season.

She walks to him and touches his arm.

No. Don't kiss me. That I do not want.

XXI

At Mark's. Len and Mark, silent.

Len What did you say?

Mark I never said anything.

Len You're at it again.

Mark It's four o'clock. I'm tired.

Len What do you do when you're tired, go to bed?

Mark That's right.

Len You sleep like a log.

Mark Of course.

Len What do you do when you wake up?

Mark Walk down the day.

Len What do you do in the day when you're not walking?

Mark I rest.

Len Where do you find a resting place?

Mark Here and there.

Len By consent?

Mark Invariably.

Len But you're not particular?

Mark Yes, I'm particular.

Len Have you a home?

Mark No.

Len So where are you?

Mark Between homes.

A distant clock chimes four.

Len Do you believe in God?

Mark What?

Len Do you believe in God?

Mark Who?

Len God.

Mark God?

Len Do you, or don't you, believe in God?

Mark Do I believe in God?

Len Yes.

Mark Would you say that again?

Len Have a biscuit.

Mark Thanks.

Len They're your biscuits. The point is, who are you? You're the sum of so many reflections. How many reflections? Whose reflections? Is that what you consist of? What scum does the tide leave? What happens to the scum? When does it happen? I've seen what happens. But I can't speak when I see it. I can only point a finger. I can't even do that. The scum is broken and sucked back. I don't see where it goes. What have I seen? What have I seen, the scum or the essence? What about it? Does all this give you the right to stand there and tell me you know who you are? It's a bloody impertinence. There's a great desert and there's a wind stopping. Perhaps you can convince me. Can you convince me? If you could only say something I could believe or begin to believe I could kill you with a clean blade and not think twice about it. But I can never kill you because you can never give me the answer I want. Neither you nor Pete. You'd both better watch out. You may be Pete's Black Knight. He may be your Black Knight. But I know one thing, and that is I'm cursed with two, two Black Knights, and until I know who you are how can I ever know who I am?

Mark That's out of order.

Len No it isn't.

Mark What's all this about Black Knights?

Len The one there. The Black Knight. Behind the curtains. Pete's yours and you're his. You live off each other.

Mark We get on like a house on fire.

Len I'm glad to hear it.

Mark All right. (*He stands.*) I've only got one thing to say.

Len Be careful.

Mark I don't know what we want. But whatever it is we won't get it.

Len Why not?

Mark Because we've got it.

Mark leaves. Len sits and closes his eyes.

XXII

Pete at home. He lets in Mark.

Mark I thought I'd take a strawzy round to see ya.

Pete Sit down. Still raining?

Mark No. Was it?

Pete Well, wasn't it?

Mark No, not for the last three quarters of an hour.

Pete You've been walking for three quarters of an hour? I didn't think you had it in you.

Mark laughs and begins to fill a pipe.

Where'd you get that?

Mark Mine. I thought I'd give it an airing.

Pete What are you smoking?

Mark Three Nuns.

Pete It's got a good pong.

Mark Yes, it makes a change.

Pete You're gassing me out.

Mark Yes, it's in good shape, this pipe. I've just given it a good clean out.

Pete Want a drink?

Mark Don't bother.

Pete Cleaning pipes, stretching your legs. Where'd you get all this energy?

Mark You've got to be able to cater, you know.

Pete Who for, women?

Mark No. I agree. There's no necessity.

Pete Mind if I smoke? (*He lights a cigarette.*) There's the rain again.

Mark You're not looking so good.

Pete As a matter of fact, things are a little topsywhatsaname at the moment.

Mark How?

Pete (*grimacing*) Aah, it's a stupid business.

Mark What's happened?

Pete Have you seen Virginia at all?

Mark Virginia? No.

Pete Well, I haven't either.

Mark Oh?

Pete She's done the dirty on me. It's finished.

Mark What's all this?

Pete She's gone down the drain. She's changed her spots.

Mark What's been going on?

Pete She's been mixing with some crowd in Soho. It's all up.

Mark I thought I hadn't seen her about.

Pete Yes, we agreed she should have a rest. For a fortnight. But she didn't come back, that's all.

Mark Well.

Pete No. If that's the way she wants it she can have it.

Mark You agreed she should have a rest?

Pete Yes. All right. Don't think I didn't see her point. I did.

Mark She needed it.

Pete Look here, Mark. She needed a rest and she got it. I tell you, she's a lost cause as far as I'm concerned. You know the kind of people she's running about with, the places she sits in? I won't even bother to describe them.

Mark But she's not your territory. How can you sanction her actions?

Pete I'm not, old boy. I'm passing my last comment on this situation.

Mark Yes, I can see your point.

Pete I've driven her to drink. All right. Let's turn over the page. I've had enough.

Pause.

Mark Should I go and see her?

Pete What for?

Mark Find out what she's up to.

Pete I've told you what she's up to.

Mark Yes, but it may not be as simple as that.

Pete What do you mean?

Mark Maybe I can do some good.

Pete Good?

Mark Find out how things really stand.

Pete In what capacity?

Mark As your friend.

Pete That's your business, if you want to see her. All I need is a breath of fresh air.

He goes to the window. Silence.

Mark Still raining.

Pete I think it's in for the night.

XXIII

Mark, at home, telephones Virginia.

Mark Virginia?
Mark.
I got your card.
I was going to phone you anyway.
What are you doing?
I'm at home.
Now?
Right. See you.

Mark prepares for Virginia's arrival. He lights the gas fire.
  Doorbell. Mark lets in Virginia.

Well, what's all this?

They sit. She crosses her legs.

Virginia All what?

Mark Pete.

Virginia There's nothing to it. It's finished.

Mark Just like that?

Virginia There's nothing else to say.

She opens her bag and takes out a packet of cigarettes. Mark stands and, bending over her chair, strikes a match. She sits back. He sits.

Mark So there's nothing else to say, eh?

Virginia It couldn't go on any longer. Have you got an ashtray?

Mark Put it in the grate.

She flicks ash into the grate and smoothes her hair over her ear. Smiles.

Virginia Tch, tch. Do you keep this place in order?

Mark Not me. A charlady.

Virginia What about the washing up?

Mark I do that.

Virginia Have you done it today?

Mark Today? No.

Virginia Shall I do it?

Mark No.

She stretches her legs and blows smoke.

Virginia I've washed up in your kitchen before.

Mark I know.

He coughs and bangs his chest.

Virginia Bad.

Mark Well, look here. You're not going back to Pete?

Virginia No. Do you take anything for that cough?

Mark No.

He clears his throat.

I hear you've been gadding about.

Virginia You could call it that.

Mark You could, eh?

Virginia I've been going about with a man called Tucker.

Mark From the West Country?

Virginia He's a Red Indian.

Mark So am I.

Virginia No you're not.

Mark What am I?

She flicks ash into the grate.

Tucker, eh?

Virginia Tucker. There's nothing else to say.

Mark Well, there must be something to say about something.

Virginia I suppose so.

Mark Give me your fag. You'll burn your fingers.

He takes the cigarette from her hand, stubs it out and sits again. He looks at her across the room.

Virginia Why are you looking at me?

Mark The same reason I always looked at you.

Virginia You're making me blush.

Mark Why did you send me that card?

Virginia I wanted to see you.

Mark Why?

Virginia Why did you phone me?

Mark I told Pete I'd phone you.

Virginia Oh?

Mark I wanted to speak to you. It's a long time since we spoke to each other.

Virginia We've hardly ever spoken to each other.

Mark Tell me.

Virginia Yes?

Mark Can you run through the snow leaving no footprint?

Virginia I think so.

Mark You must be able to do that, you know.

Virginia I think I could.

Mark Are you sure?

Virginia Don't you think I could?

Mark Yes, I do.

Virginia You knew it all the time.

Mark I've always known it. It's there, in your eyes.

Virginia Was it always there?

Mark Always. And in your body.

Virginia And in your body, too.

Mark I've never seen your legs above your knees.

Virginia No.

Mark Lift your skirt up.

Virginia Mmn?

Mark Lift your skirt up.

Virginia Like this?

Mark Yes. Go on.

Virginia Like this?

Mark Leave it.

Virginia Like this?

Mark Uncross your legs.

Virginia Like this?

Later. Virginia and Mark lie together near the glowing gas fire, after making love.

Mark Tell me.

Virginia I've told you.

Mark You've heard him say it?

Virginia From all he's ever said to me about you I don't think he respects you.

Mark He doesn't respect me and he thinks I'm a fool.

Virginia But can't you see, he doesn't respect anyone. He hates everyone.

Mark All these years, eh?

Virginia Let's forget him.

Mark scratches his head.

Mark What I can't understand is, if he thinks I'm a fool, why bother to see me?

Virginia He uses you, and everyone. (*Touching his back.*) Forget him.

Mark What sort of game has he been playing?

Virginia Look, it's all right. What the hell?

Mark What do you mean?

Virginia He hasn't harmed me. I've survived.

Mark Yes – you're all right, but there's another thing.

Virginia Look at me. Come and lie down.

Mark looks at her.

Why are you worrying so much about him?

Mark You don't understand.

Virginia He doesn't worry me any more.

Mark Do you mean to say, do you mean that after all this time with him, the cord just snaps, snap, just like that?

Virginia It was frayed.

She draws him down to her.

Do you know what I'd like now?

Mark What?

Virginia I'd like him to walk in and see us. Naked. In each other's arms.

Mark Would you?

She clasps him. He sits up.

Virginia Look, you might as well make the most of me, because we'll only last about a week.

Mark I'll tell you one thing. He's made a grave error. I'm not a fool.

XXIV

Mark's place, empty. Doorbell. Mark appears and lets in Pete.

Pete What ho. You look as if you're up to something.

Mark Don't believe it.

Pete Len's in hospital.

Mark What's the matter with him?

Pete Kidney trouble. He came a cropper.

Mark When was this?

Pete A few days ago. It's not serious.

Mark Hmmn.

Pete Well, what have you been doing with yourself?

Mark This and that.

Pete This and what?

Mark That.

Pete It sticks out a mile. Do you want to bowl along and see Len?

Mark When, now?

Pete Yes. Are you busy?

Mark No.

Pete Right.

They leave.

XXV

The streets. Mark and Pete walk, shoulders hunched.

Pete It's a fine old day. A bit chilly.

They walk on. Silence.

Done any writing lately?

Mark No.

Pete Lost the knack?

Mark I wouldn't say that.

They walk.

Pete Ah well. (*Pause.*) Read any good books lately?

Mark No.

XXVI

Pete and Mark arrive at Hackney Hospital.

Pete Here we are. Ward C.

They look around a ward.

Don't think he'd be behind a screen. Do you?

Len No hawking or canvassing!

They turn.

Pete Didn't see you.

Len (*lowering a magazine*) It's not surprising. (*They sit on each side of his bed.*) You got here.

Mark We got here.

Pete Well, what's all this?

Len I'm as right as rain now. They can't do enough for me.

Pete Why?

Len Because I'm no trouble. These nurses, they treat me like a king. Like a king. It suits me down to the ground.

Pete Staying long?

Len I'm out in two days. I'm in running order.

Mark turns to look at the nurses.

You look as though you've caught a crab.

Mark What?

Len You look undernourished.

Mark Do I?

Pete Pleasant ward.

Len It's ideal.

Mark and Pete look about the ward.

Best quality blankets, home cooking, the lot.

Mark looks up at the ceiling.

Not too low, not too high.

Pete I thought you were at death's door, when they phoned. I was going to Petticoat Lane to buy you a secondhand crucifix.

Len I told them you were my next of kin.

Len and Pete laugh. Mark is silent.

Pete By the way, Mark. What's happened to your pipe?

Mark Nothing's happened to it.

Len You smoking a pipe?

Mark No.

Pete Well, I chucked my hand in yesterday.

Len How?

Pete I gave in my notice.

Len Why?

Pete Enough's enough.

Len What are you going to do?

Pete I'm after something.

Len Let's open a business!

Silence.

Mark Well, Len, you're looking very well.

Len What's it like out?

Pete Bit chilly today.

Len Bound to be.

Pete The sun's come out.

Len That means rain.

Pete Does it?

Len Well Mark, bring off the treble chance this week?

Mark Not me.

Len Who's driving the tank?

Pete What?

Len Who's driving the tank?

Pete Don't ask me. We've been walking up the road back to back.

Len You're not supposed to sit on the bed. You're supposed to sit on the chair.

Pete (*rising*) Well, we'll leave you to it. Knock us up when you get out.

Mark (*rising*) Yes, knock us up.

Mark leaves the ward. Pete follows.

Len How do I know if you'll be in?

XXVII

Pete catches up with Mark in the street.

Pete You ever been inside one of those places?

Mark I'm not sure. I can't remember.

Pete Right. Bollocks.

They stop walking.

Mark All right. (*Scowling*.) Why do you knock on my door?

Pete What?

Mark It's a straight question.

Pete I call to see you, mate.

Mark Why?

Pete Tired of my own company.

Mark But what do you want with me? Why come and see me?

Pete Why?

Mark Either you know what you're doing or you don't know what you're doing. Either way I don't like the smell.

Pete Take it easy, Mark.

Mark I think you know bloody well what you're doing. I think you've been playing a double game for years.

Pete Don't push me, mate.

Mark You've been using me as you use every bugger. In actual fact you don't give a fuck about any of us.

Pete You've started something you might regret. But all right. Go on. Get down to brass tacks.

Mark You're two-faced. You've treated me as one thing to my face and behind my back it's been quite a different matter.

Pete Behind your back? This is infantile. Who's been pouring the poison?

Mark You've been stringing me along.

Pete I think you've got one or two things somewhat alltoballsed.

Mark Your behaviour to Virginia has been criminal for years.

Pete Watch yourself. You're out of your depth already.

Mark It's been criminal from all angles. And I'll tell you another thing, for nothing. I slept with her last night.

Silence.

Pete It's finished.

Pete walks off one way, Mark the other.

XXVIII

Later. Mark at home, slumped in a chair. He looks up and sees Pete.

Pete Are you there?

Pete comes into the room and sits.

I want you to listen.

Mark turns away.

There's something to be said. Not that you've surprised me.

Because you haven't. It's time. I'll say it. It's best. You can say what you like, if you like, afterwards. Fair enough?

What I can't sympathise with, I can only try to condone, by way of friendship. But quite frankly you must be mad, to sweep it all away in a gust of new affection.

I like the way you've painted me black. It's blunt, but erroneous.

It was a kick in the balls. I admit it. Shows I'm still subject to human pains. That's all.

No. My motives were never inspired by any great love or respect for Virginia. So you can be all the things I can't be to her. All right. Why not? I considered her a great asset to me when we had something in common, but it was very little and quite honestly very seldom.

Listen. I've liked you when you were positive, generous and friendly. When you revealed yourself. But the point is this. What have you got against me? Lies? Did I talk behind your back? The whole business is ludicrous. Of course I've spoken behind your back. Of your qualities and your faults.

I'd rather you hit me in the eye than this lark go on. Of course the whole caboodle might well be an efficient idea.

I'll add when I haven't liked you. I haven't liked you when I felt, which I did nearly all the time when we were alone, that I was a bloke you were speaking to between one bed and another.

If you know me at all, you must know that my personal relationships have nearly always been of secondary importance. My natural disposition is to be alone. It's not surprising, you see, that my friends have, however well meaning, drained my blood dry.

Perhaps I've got one knacker missing, after all.

I take it you're mortally sick of bunging your affection down a cesspool. That being in my society was an infection. Or that I've desecrated the temple.

But I believe there's more to you and me than this abortion we called friendship.

What I want you to get, above all, is that we ought to have the opportunity to blacken each other's eye, if we decide it's necessary. Also, that people like you and me, who aren't an unmixed blessing, ought to survive a love affair without being vicious, stupid or blinded.

That's it.

Mark remains still.

I suppose you've got something to say.

Mark Yes. I have. (*He turns.*) Yes, I think so. (*He looks across the room at Pete.*) My trouble is, that I have to convince myself that you don't really consider me a cunt.

So I'll assume that you don't, for the moment.

I've listened.

You see, I can appreciate, Pete, that you reserve the right to bestow contempt. So do I. But it seems to me that when it comes down to it, you inhabit a stronghold of contempt from which you can't escape.

You say friendships and whatnot have never been productive. Most of the time then, I was under a delusion. In truth you've never shared. You've been incapable. So I've been up the garden. I resent it.

The point is, are you to be treated as responsible and concerned or not? I mean, what does concern you? Surely not your friends as they wish to be, but only in so far as they can fit your requirements. Where they fail to do so, contempt, by your own logic, is the only outcome. It's their epitaph.

You've always known I was a lost cause, yet you've continued to knock on my door. Why? You couldn't work your salvation on me as you might have done on Len and Virginia, so because I was outside your moral consideration, association was permissible. You could use me as a shining example of the wrong way. As copy.

We have met. You and me. One time at a bus-stop, we were drunk. But then when you're alone? I can't trust you when you're alone.

It's what you are alone that you must be in me. Or nothing.

You've been a bloodsucker, and I think you'd do well to admit it.

Listen. The function of a friend, that you would call a friend, must be that of an ambassador to yourself, from yourself. A go-between. Then he's a man of your soul.

So you've never really got me on your kitchen staff.
I played you at the same time. It's all been a dirty
doublecross. Sure I've used you.

At the same time I know what's been good. I know
what's been real, in despite of us both. But with Virginia
nothing could stop you. You may have lost a kingdom
but it was your own destruction did it. You buggered the
issue. I was needed. Do you know that? But I took nothing
from you. It was all your own work.

You may have lost but I haven't won. That's what you
want to get into your nut.

All right. I'm willing to meet you for a cup of tea. But
I won't be your Fool and I won't be your Black Knight.

He stops, sits back, waits.

Pete Well.

His eyes screwed, he rubs his mouth.

Well, well.

I can't say how pleased I am that you recognise my
faults.

What you seem to say is that I let you down. Both of
you prefer to blame me.

But you made of your friendship a tool to bludgeon
me with and you went off and slept with Virginia. I feel
very angry about this, not without cause. I am sick,
nearly to death and to suicide, of this supposition by
Len, by Virginia, and by you most of all, that I have
anything at all to do with this cycle of love and despair
that is essentially your motive and business. I haven't.
I can help you. I can pray for you. But it's ridiculous
to think I can live with you.

If you get inside and eat my stomach I will always bite
back – in spades. Of course all I have to do to destroy
you is to leave you as you wish to be.

You've made a fool of yourself over this bed business.

The damn thing will bounce up and give you such a crack in the bollocks you won't know where it comes from.

So far as the truth is concerned, you have a lot farther to travel. If you don't think it worth it, I'm sorry. It would be many miles of good road wasted.

In the past, I haven't been able, or made it my habit, to speak the dog's honest truth about me. This time I have. You have heard it.

Silence. Pete stands.

You've got me, acid and all. On the supposition that it had to be said I've said it.

Mark coughs.

I hope the acid hasn't blinded you to the meat and salt.

Pause.

Mark I think it has.

Pete Right. I'll let myself out.

Exit Pete.

XXIX

Len walking alone, on Hackney Downs.

Len They've stopped eating. All their belongings are stacked in piles. Why are they ready for the off? I'm left in the lurch. Not even a stale frankfurter, a slice of bacon rind, a leaf of cabbage, not even a mouldy piece of salami, like they used to sling me in the days when we told old tales by suntime.

And this change. All about me the change. The yard as I know it is littered with scraps of catsmeat, pigbollocks, tincans, birdbrains, spare parts of all the little animals, a squelching squealing carpet, all the dwarfs' leavings spittled in the muck, worms stuck in the poisoned shitheaps, the alleys a whirlpool of piss, slime, blood and fruitjuice.

Now all is bare. All is clean. All is scrubbed. There is a lawn. There is a shrub. There is a flower.

Distant sound of traffic, birdsong. Lights fade.

End.